The Rise of Remote Work: A New Era of Freedom

Chapter 1: The Evolution of Work: From Office to Anywhere

In the grand tapestry of human civilization, work has always occupied a central role, adapting and evolving to meet the needs of society. The way we work has shifted dramatically over centuries, influenced by technological advancements, cultural changes, and global events. This chapter explores the historical journey that has led us to the current era of remote work, delving into key milestones, societal influences, and the implications for our future.

A Historical Perspective

To understand the rise of remote work, we must first explore the historical context in which it developed. For centuries, work was predominantly a physical endeavor, tethered to specific locations—fields, factories, and offices. The dawn of the Industrial Revolution in the late 18th century marked a significant transition in the world of work.

The Industrial Revolution and the Birth of the Office

During the Industrial Revolution, factories proliferated, drawing workers into centralized locations to contribute to mass production. The benefits of this model were evident: increased efficiency, standardized processes, and higher output. However, this system imposed rigid schedules, long hours, and often hazardous conditions, leading to widespread discontent among the workforce.

As society progressed into the early 20th century, the concept of the office as the new workplace solidified. The development of corporate structures led to the rise of the white-collar worker. Employees were expected to adhere to strict schedules, and a culture of presenteeism emerged, where workers clocked in and out, demonstrating their commitment by being physically present, regardless of productivity levels. This was further exacerbated by management theories of the time, which emphasized oversight and control to ensure productivity, often at the expense of worker satisfaction.

The Technological Revolution: Laying the Groundwork for Change

As technology advanced, so did the nature of work. The advent of computers in the 1980s, followed by the rise of the internet in the 1990s, marked the beginning of a new era. Suddenly, communication was no longer bound by geography. Email, instant messaging, and collaboration software made it possible for teams to connect and share information in real time. This technological shift laid the groundwork for remote work to emerge as a viable option.

Telecommuting began to take shape in the 1970s, but widespread acceptance remained elusive. Companies were hesitant to adopt remote work practices, often fearing a decline in productivity. However, the growing influence of technology and the changing expectations of employees gradually shifted this perception.

Cultural Shifts and the Birth of Remote Work

The cultural perception of work began to evolve in the late 20th and early 21st centuries. Increasingly, individuals sought greater work-life balance, yearning for flexibility in their professional lives. The traditional 9-to-5 model became less appealing as employees began to prioritize personal well-being alongside career aspirations. This cultural shift was driven not only by individual desires but also by a broader acknowledgment of mental health and its impact on productivity.

The concept of "work-life balance" gained traction, emphasizing the importance of integrating professional and personal responsibilities. Organizations started to recognize that employee satisfaction and well-being directly impacted productivity and retention rates.

The Pandemic as a Catalyst for Change

In 2020, the world experienced a seismic shift due to the COVID-19 pandemic. As businesses were forced to close their doors to comply with safety regulations, remote work was thrust into the spotlight. Organizations scrambled to adapt to this sudden change, and many discovered that their employees could thrive outside the confines of traditional offices.

The pandemic acted as a catalyst, accelerating the adoption of remote work and proving that productivity could be maintained, if not enhanced, in a virtual environment. Companies that had previously resisted remote work were compelled to embrace it, and many recognized the potential benefits it offered.

Key Milestones in Remote Work Evolution

Telecommuting Beginnings: The concept of telecommuting emerged in the 1970s, pioneered by companies seeking to reduce costs and provide flexibility. Early adopters began experimenting with remote work policies, though widespread acceptance remained limited.

The Internet Revolution: The proliferation of the internet in the 1990s transformed communication, enabling real-time collaboration across distances. Companies began to leverage technology to connect teams, fostering a sense of virtual community.

Remote Work Policies: By the 2010s, many organizations began to formalize remote work policies. Companies like Automattic and Buffer became pioneers in fully remote business models, proving that virtual teams could operate effectively.

The COVID-19 Pandemic: The pandemic accelerated the remote work trend, forcing millions to transition to virtual environments almost overnight. Organizations realized the potential benefits of remote work, reshaping their long-term strategies.

Hybrid Work Models: As the world recovers, hybrid work models are emerging as a dominant trend. These models combine remote and in-office work, allowing employees to choose how and where they work.

The Future of Work: Embracing Remote Work

As we look to the future, it is clear that remote work is not merely a temporary trend but a fundamental shift in how we approach our careers. The combination of technological advancements and cultural changes has created a landscape where freedom and flexibility reign. Companies that embrace this shift will not only attract top talent but also foster a culture of innovation and adaptability.

The evolution of work has brought us to a pivotal moment where remote work is a norm, not an exception. Understanding this history empowers us to navigate the challenges and opportunities that lie ahead, paving the way for a more flexible, inclusive, and dynamic future of work.

Chapter 2: The Benefits of Remote Work: Freedom and Flexibility

As remote work gains traction, it is essential to explore the numerous benefits it offers to both employees and employers. The shift from traditional office environments to remote work has redefined the way we think about productivity, work-life balance, and employee satisfaction. This chapter delves into these advantages, supported by testimonials, statistics, and case studies that illuminate the transformative potential of remote work.

Enhanced Work-Life Balance

One of the most significant advantages of remote work is the opportunity for individuals to achieve a healthier work-life balance. The elimination of daily commutes allows employees to reclaim precious hours, which can be invested in personal pursuits, family time, and self-care. A recent survey conducted by FlexJobs found that 73% of respondents cited work-life balance as the top reason for seeking remote work opportunities.

The Time Savings of Remote Work

Consider Sarah, a marketing manager who transitioned to remote work during the pandemic. "Before working from home, I spent two hours commuting each day," she recalls. "Now, I can spend that time with my kids or exercising. It's made a world of difference in my overall happiness." Sarah's experience is echoed by countless individuals who have found renewed fulfillment in their personal lives as a result of remote work.

With the elimination of commuting time, employees have the freedom to engage in activities that enrich their lives. This newfound flexibility has led to improved mental health, as individuals report lower levels of stress and greater satisfaction with their overall quality of life.

Personalized Work Environments

Remote work also allows individuals to customize their work environments to suit their preferences. For instance, some employees may thrive in quiet, minimalist spaces, while others might find inspiration in vibrant, cluttered settings. This ability to tailor one's workspace contributes to greater comfort and productivity, reinforcing the idea that happiness and well-being directly impact performance.

Increased Productivity

While some skeptics question whether remote work can maintain productivity levels, numerous studies have demonstrated that remote employees often perform at higher levels than their in-office counterparts. According to a report by Stanford University, remote workers were found to be 13% more productive than their in-office peers. This increase in productivity can be attributed to several factors:

Fewer Distractions

Remote workers can tailor their environments to minimize interruptions, leading to improved focus and output. In an office setting, distractions from coworkers, meetings, and environmental noise can hinder concentration. Remote work allows individuals to create personalized spaces that promote productivity, whether it's a quiet home office or a favorite café.

For instance, a software engineer named Mike found that working from home reduced distractions significantly. "In the office, I was constantly interrupted by people stopping by my desk. Now, I can focus on my work without those interruptions," he explains. This improved focus translates into better quality work and faster project completion.

Flexibility in Scheduling

Employees can choose when they work best, whether that be early in the morning or late at night. This autonomy fosters motivation and energy, leading to more efficient work sessions. As reported by the Buffer Remote Work Report, 32% of remote workers feel that flexibility in their schedules allows them to be more productive.

The flexibility to manage one's schedule also enables employees to address personal commitments without compromising their professional responsibilities. For example, a parent may choose to work during nap times or after their children have gone to bed, allowing them to balance both family and work obligations seamlessly.

Customized Workspaces

Many remote workers invest in creating dedicated, comfortable workspaces that cater to their unique preferences. Whether it's ergonomic furniture, natural lighting, or personalized decor, these adjustments contribute to a more conducive work environment, further enhancing productivity.

For example, Julie, a freelance graphic designer, has transformed her spare room into a vibrant studio filled with plants and artwork that inspire her creativity. "I feel more energized and focused in my workspace than I ever did in a cubicle," she shares. This sense of ownership over one's workspace can lead to heightened motivation and creativity.

Cost Savings for Employers and Employees

Remote work presents significant financial benefits for both employees and employers. For businesses, the reduction of overhead costs associated with maintaining a physical office can lead to substantial savings. According to a report by Global Workplace Analytics, companies can save an average of $11,000 per employee per year by allowing remote work.

Cost Savings for Employers

The savings for employers come from various sources:

Reduced Office Space: Companies can downsize their physical office spaces, saving on rent, utilities, and maintenance costs. This is particularly relevant in urban areas where real estate prices can be exorbitant.

For instance, a tech startup based in San Francisco reduced its office space by 50% after transitioning to a hybrid work model. The company redirected these savings toward employee development and wellness programs, enhancing overall employee satisfaction.

Lower Operational Expenses: By allowing remote work, companies can cut costs related to office supplies, technology infrastructure, and other operational expenses. This enables businesses to allocate resources more efficiently.

Higher Employee Retention: Offering remote work options can lead to increased employee satisfaction and retention, reducing the costs associated with hiring and training new employees. The expense of turnover is significant; according to the Society for Human Resource Management (SHRM), it can range from six to nine months' salary for each employee.

Cost Savings for Employees

For employees, the financial advantages are equally compelling. With no need to commute, individuals save money on gas, public transportation, and work attire. Additionally, the opportunity to work from less expensive locations can lead to substantial cost reductions. Many remote workers have chosen to relocate from high-cost urban areas to more affordable suburban or rural regions, allowing them to stretch their salaries further.

John, a remote software developer, moved from New York City to a small town in Vermont, where the cost of living is significantly lower. "I'm able to live comfortably and save money while doing the same job," he states. This shift not only improved his financial situation but also enhanced his quality of life.

Access to a Global Talent Pool

The rise of remote work has dismantled geographical barriers, enabling companies to tap into a global talent pool. Organizations are no longer confined to hiring talent within a specific radius of their offices, which enhances diversity and fosters innovation. This is particularly advantageous for businesses seeking specialized skills that may not be readily available locally.

Diversity and Inclusion

Hiring remotely allows organizations to build diverse teams, drawing on varied perspectives and experiences that contribute to innovation and problem-solving. A McKinsey report found that companies with diverse workforces are 35% more likely to outperform their competitors.

For example, a marketing agency based in London has successfully hired remote employees from diverse backgrounds across the globe. This diversity enriches the agency's creative processes, enabling them to develop more inclusive and innovative marketing campaigns.

The Future of Work: Embracing Remote Work

As we move forward into an increasingly digital future, remote work will likely become the norm rather than the exception. Organizations that embrace flexibility, autonomy, and diversity will be better positioned to attract and retain top talent in a competitive job market.

In conclusion, the benefits of remote work extend far beyond individual convenience; they encompass enhanced productivity, cost savings, and the potential for diverse and innovative teams. As businesses and employees alike recognize the advantages of this new way of working, remote work is set to redefine the future landscape of employment.

Chapter 3: Overcoming Challenges: Navigating Remote Work Hurdles

While the benefits of remote work are abundant, it is essential to acknowledge and address the challenges that come with this shift. Remote work introduces unique hurdles that both employees and employers must navigate to ensure a successful transition. This chapter explores common challenges, practical solutions, and strategies for fostering a thriving remote work culture.

Isolation and Loneliness

One of the most significant challenges remote workers face is feelings of isolation and loneliness. Without the daily interactions that occur in an office setting, individuals may struggle to build connections with colleagues. A survey conducted by Buffer found that 20% of remote workers cited loneliness as their primary struggle.

Building Connections in a Remote Environment

To combat loneliness, organizations must foster a sense of community among remote teams. Virtual team-building activities, regular check-ins, and informal gatherings can help create connections and camaraderie. For instance, many companies now organize virtual happy hours, game nights, or book clubs to encourage social interaction.

Encouraging Open Communication

Establishing open lines of communication is vital in a remote work environment. Employers should encourage employees to share their experiences and feelings, creating a culture of support. Regular one-on-one meetings and team huddles can provide opportunities for employees to voice concerns, share successes, and connect with one another.

In addition, tools like Slack, Microsoft Teams, or Zoom can facilitate real-time communication, allowing employees to reach out to colleagues easily. Creating dedicated channels for casual conversations or sharing personal updates can help foster a sense of community.

Communication Challenges

Remote work can create barriers to effective communication, leading to misunderstandings and decreased productivity. The absence of non-verbal cues, such as body language and facial expressions, can make it difficult to convey messages accurately. A study by the Harvard Business Review found that remote teams often experience communication breakdowns due to misinterpretation of tone and context.

Establishing Clear Communication Protocols

To mitigate communication challenges, organizations should establish clear communication protocols. This includes guidelines for response times, preferred communication channels, and expectations for availability. For instance, companies may choose to designate specific hours for synchronous communication while allowing for asynchronous updates throughout the day.

Leveraging Technology for Collaboration

Utilizing collaboration tools is essential for maintaining effective communication in remote work settings. Project management software, video conferencing, and shared document platforms can facilitate collaboration and keep teams aligned. Tools like Trello, Asana, or Google Workspace can help teams track progress, share feedback, and manage projects seamlessly.

Regularly scheduled video meetings can also help bridge the gap created by remote work. Face-to-face interactions, even through screens, can enhance understanding and connection among team members. Additionally, employers should encourage employees to turn on their cameras during meetings, promoting engagement and a sense of presence.

Work-Life Boundaries

Remote work blurs the lines between personal and professional life, making it challenging for employees to establish clear boundaries. Many remote workers report feeling the need to be "always on," leading to burnout and decreased job satisfaction.

Encouraging Work-Life Balance

To address this challenge, employers should promote a culture of work-life balance. Encouraging employees to set designated work hours, take regular breaks, and disconnect after hours can help create a healthier work environment. Companies can lead by example, with leaders demonstrating healthy boundaries themselves.

Promoting Mental Health Awareness

Employers should also prioritize mental health resources for remote employees. This may include access to counseling services, wellness programs, or mindfulness workshops. By fostering an environment that values mental health, organizations can help employees navigate the challenges of remote work more effectively.

Performance Measurement

Assessing employee performance in a remote work environment can be challenging, particularly when traditional metrics centered on visibility and presenteeism may no longer apply. Employers may struggle to determine how to evaluate productivity and ensure accountability without micromanaging.

Implementing Goal-Oriented Metrics

To address this issue, organizations should shift to goal-oriented performance metrics. By focusing on outcomes rather than hours worked, employers can create a culture of trust and empowerment. Setting clear objectives and key results (OKRs) can provide employees with a roadmap for success while allowing them the autonomy to achieve their goals in their own way.

Encouraging Regular Feedback

Regular feedback is essential for supporting employee growth and development. Organizations should establish a feedback culture that encourages ongoing conversations between managers and employees. This can include formal performance reviews, as well as informal check-ins to discuss progress, challenges, and opportunities for improvement.

Conclusion

Navigating the challenges of remote work requires intentional effort and a commitment to fostering a supportive and inclusive culture. By addressing issues such as isolation, communication barriers, work-life boundaries, and performance measurement, organizations can create a thriving remote work environment that benefits both employees and employers.

As we embrace this new era of work, it is crucial to remember that flexibility and adaptability are key. The challenges of remote work are not insurmountable; they can be transformed into opportunities for growth, collaboration, and innovation. By cultivating a culture that values connection, communication, and well-being, organizations can ensure that remote work remains a viable and rewarding option for the future.

Chapter 4: The Tools of the Trade: Essential Technology for Remote Work

In the world of remote work, technology plays a pivotal role in facilitating communication, collaboration, and productivity. As employees transition to virtual environments, having access to the right tools is essential for success. This chapter explores the essential technology for remote work, highlighting various tools, platforms, and best practices that can enhance the remote work experience.

Communication Tools

Effective communication is the cornerstone of successful remote work. Without the ability to connect in person, remote teams must rely on various communication tools to collaborate effectively. Here are some essential communication tools:

Video Conferencing Platforms

Video conferencing software has become indispensable for remote teams. Tools like Zoom, Microsoft Teams, and Google Meet enable face-to-face interactions, fostering connection and collaboration. These platforms allow teams to conduct meetings, presentations, and brainstorming sessions, replicating the in-person experience as closely as possible.

Consider Emily, a project manager who leads a remote team spread across multiple time zones. "Video calls have been a game-changer for us," she explains. "Being able to see each other's faces fosters a sense of connection and allows us to read non-verbal cues, which is crucial for effective communication."

Instant Messaging Applications

Instant messaging tools, such as Slack or Microsoft Teams, facilitate real-time communication and quick updates. These platforms allow team members to chat, share files, and collaborate on projects in a dynamic environment. Channels can be created for specific teams or projects, enabling focused discussions without the need for lengthy email threads.

For example, a remote marketing team uses Slack to communicate about ongoing campaigns. "We have dedicated channels for each project, making it easy to share ideas and get feedback quickly," shares Jake, a marketing strategist. This immediate access to information and colleagues promotes efficiency and collaboration.

Project Management Software

Managing projects and tasks effectively is vital in a remote work environment. Project management software provides teams with a centralized platform to track progress, assign tasks, and collaborate on projects.

Task Management Tools

Tools like Trello, Asana, and Monday.com enable teams to visualize their workflows, set deadlines, and monitor task completion. These platforms promote accountability and transparency, ensuring that everyone is on the same page.

For instance, a remote software development team uses Trello to manage their sprints. Each team member can see the status of tasks, provide updates, and move cards through different stages of completion. "It helps us stay organized and accountable, even though we're not physically together," explains Alex, a software developer.

Document Collaboration

Collaboration on documents is another critical aspect of remote work. Tools like Google Workspace and Microsoft Office 365 enable teams to create, edit, and share documents in real time. This fosters collaboration and ensures that everyone has access to the most up-to-date information.

For example, a remote writing team uses Google Docs to draft and edit articles together. "We can see each other's changes in real time, which speeds up the writing process and enhances collaboration," shares Rachel, a content writer.

Time Management and Productivity Tools

Maintaining productivity in a remote work environment requires effective time management. Various tools can help employees track their time, set goals, and stay focused.

Time Tracking Software

Time tracking tools like Toggl and Harvest allow employees to monitor how they spend their time throughout the day. By understanding where their time goes, individuals can identify areas for improvement and optimize their workflows.

For instance, a remote consultant named Laura uses Toggl to track her hours spent on client projects. "It helps me see which tasks are taking longer than expected, allowing me to adjust my strategies accordingly," she explains. This self-awareness leads to improved efficiency and better time management.

Focus and Productivity Apps

Productivity apps, such as Focus@Will or Forest, help remote workers maintain focus and minimize distractions. These tools often employ techniques like the Pomodoro Technique, which encourages users to work in focused bursts followed by short breaks.

A remote graphic designer named Mark finds that using the Forest app helps him stay on track. "When I see my virtual forest growing, it motivates me to stay focused on my tasks," he shares. This gamified approach to productivity encourages individuals to minimize distractions and maximize efficiency.

Cybersecurity and Data Protection

As remote work becomes increasingly prevalent, cybersecurity is a paramount concern. Organizations must prioritize data protection to safeguard sensitive information and maintain the integrity of their systems.

Virtual Private Networks (VPNs)

VPNs provide an additional layer of security for remote workers by encrypting internet connections. This is particularly important for employees accessing company networks from public Wi-Fi, where data breaches are more likely to occur. Organizations should encourage employees to use VPNs when working remotely to protect sensitive information.

Password Management Tools

Password management tools, such as LastPass or 1Password, help employees create and store secure passwords for various applications. With the increasing number of accounts individuals need to manage, these tools enhance security by promoting the use of strong, unique passwords.

Conclusion

In the realm of remote work, technology is the backbone that supports communication, collaboration, and productivity. By leveraging the right tools, organizations can empower their remote teams to thrive, fostering a culture of innovation and adaptability.

As remote work continues to evolve, it is essential for businesses to stay informed about emerging technologies and best practices. Investing in the right tools not only enhances employee satisfaction but also contributes to the overall success of the organization. In this new era of work, the right technology can make all the difference in creating a productive, engaged, and connected workforce.

Chapter 5: The Future of Remote Work: Trends and Predictions

As the world of work continues to evolve, the future of remote work holds exciting possibilities. The experiences gained during the COVID-19 pandemic have reshaped perceptions of remote work, prompting organizations to reconsider their approaches to flexibility, collaboration, and employee engagement. This chapter explores emerging trends and predictions for the future of remote work, highlighting key factors that will influence this ongoing transformation.

Hybrid Work Models: The New Normal

One of the most significant trends shaping the future of work is the rise of hybrid work models. Companies are increasingly adopting flexible arrangements that allow employees to split their time between remote and in-office work. This approach combines the benefits of both environments, catering to diverse employee preferences and fostering collaboration.

The Flexibility Advantage

Hybrid work models offer employees the flexibility to choose when and where they work, leading to increased job satisfaction. According to a recent survey by Gartner, 82% of company leaders plan to allow employees to work remotely at least part of the time. This shift acknowledges the diverse needs of the workforce, accommodating individuals who thrive in different environments.

Reimagining Office Spaces

As hybrid work becomes more prevalent, organizations are rethinking their office spaces. Traditional cubicle setups are giving way to collaborative spaces designed for teamwork and creativity. These reimagined environments prioritize flexibility, with movable furniture, open areas for brainstorming, and quiet zones for focused work.

For instance, a tech company in Silicon Valley has transformed its office into a collaborative hub, featuring lounge areas, brainstorming rooms, and dedicated spaces for virtual meetings. Employees are encouraged to come into the office for team collaboration and social interaction, while also having the option to work remotely when it suits their needs.

Technology-Driven Solutions

The future of remote work will be heavily influenced by advancements in technology. As organizations continue to embrace digital solutions, innovative tools will emerge to enhance collaboration, communication, and productivity.

Artificial Intelligence and Automation

Artificial intelligence (AI) and automation will play a crucial role in shaping the future of remote work. These technologies can streamline repetitive tasks, enhance decision-making processes, and improve collaboration among remote teams. For example, AI-powered tools can analyze employee productivity patterns and suggest personalized work schedules that maximize efficiency.

Virtual Reality (VR) and Augmented Reality (AR)

Virtual and augmented reality technologies hold tremendous potential for remote collaboration. These immersive technologies can create virtual meeting spaces where employees can interact as if they were in the same room. For example, a remote design team can collaborate in a virtual environment, manipulating 3D models and discussing changes in real time.

While VR and AR are still in their infancy, their integration into remote work practices could revolutionize the way teams collaborate, enhancing engagement and interaction.

Focus on Employee Well-Being

As remote work continues to evolve, organizations will increasingly prioritize employee well-being. The importance of mental health and work-life balance will take center stage, leading to the implementation of policies and practices that support employees' overall health.

Wellness Programs and Resources

Employers will invest in wellness programs that promote physical and mental well-being. This may include access to fitness classes, mental health resources, and mindfulness workshops. Organizations that prioritize employee well-being will foster a positive work culture, leading to increased engagement and productivity.

Encouraging Disconnecting

With the blurred boundaries between work and personal life, companies will emphasize the importance of disconnecting after work hours. Encouraging employees to unplug from their devices and take breaks will be vital for preventing burnout and maintaining a healthy work-life balance.

Diversity, Equity, and Inclusion

Remote work has the potential to foster greater diversity, equity, and inclusion (DEI) in the workplace. As organizations expand their talent pools to include individuals from various backgrounds, they can build more inclusive teams that drive innovation.

Addressing Bias in Remote Work

While remote work offers opportunities for greater inclusion, organizations must actively address potential biases that may arise in virtual environments. This includes creating equitable processes for hiring, promotions, and performance evaluations. Companies should implement training programs to raise awareness of unconscious bias and promote inclusive practices among remote teams.

Conclusion

The future of remote work is filled with promise and potential. As organizations adapt to hybrid work models, leverage emerging technologies, and prioritize employee well-being, the landscape of work will continue to evolve.

By embracing flexibility, fostering collaboration, and promoting diversity and inclusion, organizations can create thriving remote work environments that empower employees and drive success. As we look ahead, it is clear that remote work is not just a temporary trend; it is a fundamental shift in how we approach our careers, paving the way for a more flexible, innovative, and inclusive future of work.

Chapter 6: Strategies for Success: Building a Remote Work Culture

The success of remote work relies not only on technology and policies but also on cultivating a strong organizational culture that fosters connection, collaboration, and engagement. In this chapter, we will explore effective strategies for building a thriving remote work culture, highlighting best practices for leaders and employees alike.

Defining Company Values and Vision

A strong remote work culture begins with clearly defined company values and vision. Organizations should articulate their mission, goals, and core values, ensuring that all employees understand and align with these principles. A shared sense of purpose fosters a sense of belonging and motivates employees to contribute meaningfully to the organization.

Communicating Values Effectively

Leaders should communicate company values through various channels, including onboarding materials, team meetings, and internal communications. Regular discussions about values can reinforce their importance and encourage employees to embody them in their work.

For example, a remote startup emphasizes its commitment to collaboration and innovation through weekly team meetings where employees share ideas and celebrate successes. This reinforces a culture of openness and creativity.

Fostering Open Communication

Open communication is essential for building a strong remote work culture. Organizations should create an environment where employees feel comfortable sharing their thoughts, concerns, and feedback.

Encouraging Transparency

Leaders should promote transparency by sharing information about company performance, decisions, and changes. Regular updates, town hall meetings, and open forums can provide opportunities for employees to engage with leadership and ask questions.

In addition, organizations can leverage communication tools to facilitate feedback and idea-sharing. Anonymous surveys or suggestion boxes can encourage employees to voice their opinions without fear of repercussions.

Building Trust and Accountability

Trust is the foundation of a successful remote work culture. Leaders must cultivate trust among team members by demonstrating reliability, consistency, and integrity.

Empowering Employees

To build trust, organizations should empower employees to take ownership of their work. This includes granting autonomy in decision-making and encouraging individuals to take initiative. When employees feel trusted to make choices, they are more likely to be engaged and motivated.

For instance, a remote consulting firm allows employees to set their own project timelines, fostering a sense of ownership and accountability. "Having the freedom to manage my own schedule has made me more committed to my work," shares Sarah, a consultant.

Recognizing and Celebrating Achievements

Recognizing and celebrating employee achievements is crucial for fostering motivation and engagement. Remote work can sometimes lead to feelings of isolation, making it important for organizations to acknowledge contributions and successes.

Implementing Recognition Programs

Organizations can establish recognition programs that highlight individual and team accomplishments. This may include employee of the month awards, shout-outs during meetings, or recognition on internal communication channels. Celebrating successes reinforces a positive culture and encourages continued effort.

For example, a remote sales team celebrates quarterly achievements with virtual awards ceremonies, where top performers are recognized for their contributions. "It's great to be acknowledged for our hard work, especially when working remotely," says Mark, a sales representative.

Encouraging Professional Development

Investing in employee growth and development is essential for fostering a strong remote work culture. Organizations should prioritize learning opportunities that empower employees to enhance their skills and advance their careers.

Providing Training and Resources

Employers can offer access to online training programs, workshops, and mentorship opportunities. Encouraging continuous learning not only benefits employees but also contributes to the organization's success.

For instance, a remote tech company provides access to online courses and professional development resources. Employees are encouraged to pursue certifications and training that align with their career goals. "The company supports my growth, and it's motivating to know that they care about my development," shares David, a software engineer.

Conclusion

Building a thriving remote work culture requires intentional effort and a commitment to fostering connection, collaboration, and engagement. By defining company values, promoting open communication, building trust, recognizing achievements, and investing in professional development, organizations can create a positive remote work environment that empowers employees to thrive.

As we move forward in the remote work era, organizations must prioritize culture as a fundamental aspect of their success. A strong remote work culture not only enhances employee satisfaction but also drives productivity, innovation, and overall organizational success. By embracing these strategies, organizations can create a vibrant remote work culture that supports employees and positions them for future success.

Chapter 7: Navigating Challenges in Remote Work

While remote work offers numerous benefits, it also presents unique challenges that individuals and organizations must navigate to ensure success. This chapter examines the common obstacles associated with remote work and provides practical strategies for overcoming them.

1. Combatting Isolation and Loneliness

One of the most significant challenges of remote work is the potential for feelings of isolation and loneliness. Without the daily interactions that occur in a traditional office, employees may miss the social connections that foster a sense of belonging.

The Impact of Isolation

Studies indicate that loneliness can negatively affect mental health and job performance. A report from the American Psychological Association (APA) highlights that loneliness can lead to decreased motivation, increased stress levels, and lower overall job satisfaction.

Strategies for Connection

To combat isolation, organizations can implement strategies that foster connection among remote employees. Regular virtual team-building activities, such as online games or social hours, can create opportunities for informal interactions and strengthen relationships.

For example, a remote marketing agency hosts monthly virtual happy hours where team members share personal updates and participate in fun activities. "These gatherings help us feel more connected, even if we're miles apart," shares Lucy, a marketing coordinator.

2. Managing Work-Life Balance

The blurring of boundaries between work and personal life is another challenge of remote work. Employees may find it difficult to "switch off," leading to longer hours and increased stress.

The Risks of Overwork

Research by Gallup shows that remote workers often log more hours than their in-office counterparts. The lack of a clear separation between work and home life can contribute to burnout and decreased productivity over time.

Creating Boundaries

Organizations can help employees establish healthy work-life boundaries by promoting policies that encourage taking breaks and respecting time off. For instance, companies can set expectations around communication after hours and encourage employees to create designated workspaces at home.

A remote software company implements a "no emails after 6 PM" policy to help employees disconnect and recharge. "This policy has made a significant difference in my work-life balance," explains Tom, a software engineer.

3. Ensuring Effective Communication

Effective communication is essential for remote teams to function smoothly. However, miscommunications can occur more easily when team members are not in the same physical space.

Common Communication Pitfalls

Misinterpretations of tone, delayed responses, and lack of non-verbal cues can lead to misunderstandings among remote workers. A study by the Journal of Business and Technical Communication found that remote teams face unique communication challenges that can hinder collaboration.

Enhancing Communication Practices

To improve communication, organizations should establish clear guidelines for communication protocols. Regular check-ins, video calls, and collaborative tools can enhance interactions and ensure everyone is on the same page.

For instance, a remote design team conducts daily stand-up meetings to discuss progress and address challenges. "These meetings help us stay aligned and foster a collaborative spirit," notes Sarah, a graphic designer.

4. Addressing Performance and Accountability

Measuring employee performance in a remote work environment can be challenging. Traditional methods of evaluation may not effectively capture individual contributions and outcomes.

The Shift in Performance Metrics

Organizations need to shift their focus from monitoring hours worked to assessing results and outcomes. This change requires a reevaluation of how success is defined and measured.

Implementing Performance Metrics

To foster accountability, companies can set clear performance goals and outcomes for employees. Regular feedback sessions and performance reviews can provide opportunities for constructive discussions about progress and areas for improvement.

For example, a remote consulting firm utilizes a performance dashboard that tracks key performance indicators (KPIs) for each employee. This transparency promotes accountability and encourages continuous improvement.

5. Dealing with Technology Dependence

Remote work heavily relies on technology for communication, collaboration, and productivity. However, technical issues can disrupt workflows and lead to frustration.

The Risks of Over-Reliance on Technology

As remote work increases reliance on digital tools, employees may experience "Zoom fatigue" or become overwhelmed by constant notifications. A report from Microsoft reveals that remote workers spend an average of 10 hours a week in virtual meetings, which can lead to burnout.

Balancing Technology Use

Organizations should encourage a balanced approach to technology. Limiting the number of meetings, promoting asynchronous communication, and providing training on effective tool usage can enhance productivity and reduce stress.

A remote education company has adopted a "meeting-free Fridays" policy to give employees uninterrupted time to focus on their work. "It's refreshing to have a day dedicated to deep work," says Anna, an instructional designer.

Conclusion

While remote work presents challenges, organizations can implement effective strategies to navigate these obstacles. By prioritizing connection, establishing boundaries, enhancing communication, measuring performance, and balancing technology use, companies can create a supportive environment that fosters employee success and satisfaction.

Chapter 8: Building a Remote-Friendly Organization

To fully embrace the benefits of remote work, organizations must develop a remote-friendly culture that supports employees and promotes collaboration. This chapter explores the key components of building a remote-friendly organization and highlights best practices for leaders.

1. Emphasizing Trust and Autonomy

A successful remote-friendly organization is built on a foundation of trust and autonomy. Leaders must empower employees to take ownership of their work, fostering an environment where individuals feel valued and trusted.

Cultivating a Culture of Trust

Trust is established through transparency and accountability. Leaders should communicate openly about company goals, expectations, and performance metrics, allowing employees to understand their contributions to the organization's success.

For example, a remote tech startup conducts regular town hall meetings where leadership shares updates and encourages questions from employees. "This level of transparency makes me feel like I'm part of something bigger," says Jenna, a project manager.

2. Prioritizing Employee Well-Being

Employee well-being is crucial for a thriving remote-friendly organization. Leaders must recognize the importance of mental health and provide resources that support employees' overall well-being.

Implementing Wellness Initiatives

Organizations can implement wellness initiatives that promote physical and mental health. This may include access to fitness programs, mental health resources, and flexible scheduling to accommodate personal needs.

A remote consulting firm offers virtual fitness classes and mental health workshops, ensuring employees have access to resources that support their well-being. "These initiatives have made a positive impact on my overall health," shares Ethan, a consultant.

3. Fostering Collaboration and Innovation

Collaboration is essential for driving innovation and creativity in a remote-friendly organization. Leaders should create opportunities for cross-functional collaboration and encourage team members to share ideas.

Creating Collaborative Spaces

Virtual collaboration tools, such as brainstorming platforms and shared project management systems, can facilitate innovation. Organizations should encourage employees to collaborate across teams and departments to leverage diverse perspectives and expertise.

A remote design agency utilizes a shared digital whiteboard for brainstorming sessions, allowing team members to contribute ideas in real-time. "This collaborative environment fosters creativity and encourages us to think outside the box," explains Lisa, a UX designer.

4. Encouraging Continuous Learning and Development

A remote-friendly organization prioritizes continuous learning and development, ensuring employees have access to resources that enhance their skills and knowledge.

Investing in Professional Development

Organizations should provide opportunities for professional growth, such as training programs, mentorship, and access to online courses. This investment not only benefits employees but also contributes to the organization's success.

A remote marketing firm offers a stipend for employees to pursue professional development opportunities, whether it's attending conferences or enrolling in online courses. "Having access to learning resources keeps me engaged and motivated," says Ryan, a marketing specialist.

5. Celebrating Diversity and Inclusion

A remote-friendly organization values diversity and inclusion, recognizing the importance of diverse perspectives in driving innovation. Leaders must prioritize DEI initiatives and create a culture that embraces individuals from various backgrounds.

Implementing Inclusive Practices

Organizations can implement inclusive practices by providing diversity training, establishing employee resource groups, and ensuring equitable opportunities for all employees. Creating a culture of inclusion fosters a sense of belonging and engagement among remote workers.

A remote nonprofit organization has established employee resource groups that focus on supporting underrepresented communities within the workplace. "These groups provide a space for us to share our experiences and promote inclusivity," shares Maria, a program manager.

Conclusion

Building a remote-friendly organization requires intentional effort and a commitment to fostering trust, well-being, collaboration, learning, and inclusion. By prioritizing these key components, organizations can create a thriving remote work environment that empowers employees and drives success.

Chapter 9: Legal Considerations for Remote Work

As remote work becomes increasingly common, organizations must navigate various legal considerations to ensure compliance and protect their interests. This chapter explores the legal aspects of remote work and provides guidance for organizations to navigate this evolving landscape.

1. Employment Laws and Regulations

Organizations must be aware of employment laws and regulations that apply to remote workers. These laws may vary by jurisdiction and can impact areas such as wage and hour regulations, employee classification, and benefits.

Understanding Wage and Hour Laws

Remote work does not exempt organizations from wage and hour laws. Employers must ensure compliance with regulations related to overtime, minimum wage, and meal breaks.

For example, organizations should track the hours worked by remote employees accurately, especially for non-exempt workers. This may involve implementing time-tracking software or requiring regular timesheet submissions to ensure compliance.

2. Employee Classification

Properly classifying employees is crucial for compliance with labor laws. Organizations must determine whether workers are classified as employees or independent contractors, as this distinction impacts benefits, taxes, and liability.

Assessing Worker Classification

Employers should review the relationship between the organization and its workers to ensure compliance with classification criteria. Misclassification can lead to legal disputes and financial penalties.

For instance, a remote graphic design firm must assess whether freelancers are classified as independent contractors or employees based on the level of control and independence in their work. "Understanding the classification helps protect both the company and the worker," notes Karen, an HR manager.

3. Privacy and Data Security

Remote work raises concerns regarding data privacy and security. Organizations must implement measures to protect sensitive information and comply with data protection regulations.

Implementing Data Protection Policies

Employers should establish data protection policies that outline best practices for handling sensitive information. This may include training employees on data security measures, implementing encryption, and using secure communication channels.

A remote financial services firm conducts regular training sessions on data security to ensure employees understand their responsibilities in protecting client information. "Staying informed about data security is crucial for our clients' trust," shares James, a compliance officer.

4. Workplace Safety and Ergonomics

Although employees are working from home, organizations still have a responsibility to ensure workplace safety and ergonomics. Employers should provide resources and guidance to help employees create safe and ergonomic home workspaces.

Establishing Ergonomics Guidelines

Organizations can provide resources on ergonomics best practices, such as setting up a home office, proper seating arrangements, and break schedules. Employers may also consider offering stipends for ergonomic equipment.

A remote tech company provides employees with guidelines on creating an ergonomic workspace and offers stipends for purchasing ergonomic furniture. "Having a comfortable workspace has improved my productivity," notes Rachel, a software developer.

5. Establishing Remote Work Policies

Developing clear remote work policies is essential for setting expectations and ensuring compliance. These policies should address various aspects of remote work, including communication, performance expectations, and data security.

Crafting Comprehensive Remote Work Policies

Organizations should involve employees in the policy development process to ensure buy-in and address concerns. Policies should be easily accessible and regularly updated to reflect changes in the remote work landscape.

A remote consulting firm conducts regular reviews of its remote work policies and seeks employee feedback to ensure relevance and effectiveness. "Being part of the policy development process makes us feel valued," shares Amy, a consultant.

Conclusion

Navigating the legal considerations of remote work requires vigilance and proactive measures. By understanding employment laws, ensuring proper classification, protecting data, prioritizing safety, and establishing clear policies, organizations can mitigate legal risks and create a compliant remote work environment.

Chapter 10: The Future of Remote Work

As remote work continues to evolve, organizations must anticipate future trends and adapt their strategies to thrive in an increasingly remote-centric world. This chapter explores the future of remote work, highlighting emerging trends and predictions for the workplace.

1. Hybrid Work Models

The future of work is likely to embrace hybrid models that combine remote and in-office work. Organizations will need to navigate the complexities of managing a distributed workforce while maintaining a cohesive culture.

The Benefits of Hybrid Work

Hybrid work models offer flexibility, allowing employees to choose where and when they work. This approach can lead to increased employee satisfaction, retention, and productivity.

For instance, a remote-first company may adopt a hybrid model, allowing employees to work remotely for most of the week while coming into the office for team meetings and collaboration. "This flexibility allows me to balance my work and personal life effectively," explains Kevin, a project manager.

2. Advancements in Technology

Emerging technologies will continue to play a significant role in shaping the future of remote work. Organizations will need to stay informed about advancements that enhance collaboration, communication, and productivity.

Embracing New Tools

As new tools and platforms emerge, organizations should evaluate their potential to improve remote work experiences. Virtual reality (VR) and augmented reality (AR) technologies may offer innovative ways to facilitate collaboration and engagement.

A remote design firm is exploring VR tools for virtual brainstorming sessions, allowing team members to collaborate in a virtual space. "These technologies have the potential to revolutionize how we work together," notes Rachel, a design lead.

3. Evolving Workplace Culture

The cultural dynamics of remote work will continue to evolve. Organizations must prioritize creating an inclusive and engaging culture that supports diverse teams, regardless of their physical location.

Fostering Inclusivity

To build a strong remote culture, organizations should implement initiatives that promote diversity and inclusion. This may involve training programs, mentorship opportunities, and employee resource groups that cater to diverse needs.

A remote nonprofit organization has established a diversity task force that focuses on promoting inclusion within the remote workforce. "Creating a culture of inclusivity is essential for our success," shares Naomi, the executive director.

4. Focus on Employee Well-Being

As the remote work landscape evolves, organizations must prioritize employee well-being as a core aspect of their strategies. Mental health resources, flexible schedules, and wellness initiatives will be crucial for supporting employees.

Implementing Well-Being Programs

Organizations can develop comprehensive well-being programs that address mental, physical, and emotional health.

This may include access to counseling services, fitness initiatives, and opportunities for social connection.

A remote tech company offers a comprehensive wellness program that includes mental health days, fitness challenges, and regular check-ins with wellness coaches. "Knowing that my well-being is a priority makes a significant difference," shares Jenna, a software engineer.

5. The Role of Leadership in Shaping the Future

Leaders will play a vital role in shaping the future of remote work. Organizations must invest in leadership development to equip leaders with the skills needed to manage remote teams effectively.

Developing Remote Leadership Skills

Leadership development programs should focus on building skills related to communication, trust-building, and employee engagement in remote settings. Effective leaders will foster a culture of collaboration and accountability, driving team success.

A remote consulting firm offers leadership training programs that emphasize remote management skills and strategies for fostering engagement. "Investing in leadership development ensures that our leaders are equipped to navigate the challenges of remote work," notes Eric, the head of HR.

Conclusion

The future of remote work presents both challenges and opportunities for organizations. By embracing hybrid work models, leveraging technology, fostering inclusivity, prioritizing well-being, and investing in leadership development, organizations can thrive in the evolving landscape of remote work.

As we move forward, it is essential to remain adaptable and open to change, recognizing that the future of work is a collaborative journey that requires collective effort and innovation. Together, we can shape a future where remote work enhances our careers and lives.

Chapter 11: Leveraging Remote Work for Global Talent Acquisition

Remote work has opened doors to a global talent pool, allowing organizations to tap into diverse skills and perspectives from around the world. This chapter explores how organizations can leverage remote work for talent acquisition and build high-performing teams.

1. Expanding the Talent Pool

The traditional limitations of geographical boundaries are no longer a barrier for organizations seeking talent. Remote work enables companies to hire the best candidates, regardless of their location.

The Benefits of a Diverse Workforce

A diverse workforce can lead to increased creativity, innovation, and problem-solving capabilities. Research by McKinsey & Company shows that organizations with diverse teams are more likely to outperform their peers in profitability and value creation.

For instance, a remote tech startup recently hired software engineers from different countries, bringing diverse perspectives and ideas to the team. "Having a global team enriches our work and allows us to approach problems from various angles," shares Mark, the CTO.

2. Implementing Global Recruitment Strategies

To attract top talent globally, organizations must develop recruitment strategies that resonate with diverse candidates. This may involve tailoring job descriptions, using inclusive language, and showcasing the company culture.

Utilizing Online Platforms

Leveraging online job platforms, social media, and professional networks can help organizations reach a wider audience. Creating engaging employer branding materials can also enhance the organization's appeal to prospective candidates.

A remote marketing agency utilizes platforms like LinkedIn and Glassdoor to showcase employee testimonials and company values, attracting candidates who align with their culture. "Highlighting our remote culture has helped us connect with the right talent," notes Sarah, the HR manager.

3. Navigating Cultural Differences

When building a global remote team, organizations must be aware of cultural differences that may impact communication, collaboration, and work styles.

Promoting Cultural Awareness

Organizations should provide training and resources to promote cultural awareness among team members. Understanding cultural differences fosters respect and enhances collaboration within diverse teams.

A remote consulting firm conducts regular cultural awareness workshops, allowing employees to learn about their colleagues' backgrounds and work styles. "These workshops have helped us communicate better and appreciate each other's perspectives," shares Ahmed, a consultant.

4. Creating an Inclusive Onboarding Experience

An inclusive onboarding experience is crucial for integrating new remote employees into the organization. This process should focus on fostering connection, engagement, and belonging.

Implementing a Comprehensive Onboarding Program

Organizations can develop onboarding programs that introduce new hires to the company culture, values, and expectations. Assigning mentors or buddies can also provide new employees with guidance and support during their transition.

A remote tech company offers a structured onboarding program that includes virtual meet-and-greets with team members and training sessions on company tools and processes. "Having a supportive onboarding experience made my transition smooth," notes Jennifer, a new software engineer.

5. Fostering Collaboration Across Time Zones

Remote teams often span multiple time zones, which can create challenges for collaboration. Organizations must implement strategies that facilitate effective communication and teamwork among team members located in different regions.

Utilizing Time Zone Tools

Employing time zone tools can help teams schedule meetings at convenient times for all participants. Establishing core hours when team members are available can also enhance collaboration.

A remote marketing firm utilizes a shared calendar tool that displays team members' time zones, making it easier to coordinate meetings and collaborate effectively. "This tool has eliminated confusion around scheduling and has improved our teamwork," shares Laura, a marketing specialist.

Conclusion

Leveraging remote work for global talent acquisition presents exciting opportunities for organizations to build diverse, high-performing teams. By expanding the talent pool, implementing inclusive recruitment strategies, promoting cultural awareness, creating engaging onboarding experiences, and fostering collaboration across time zones, organizations can unlock the potential of remote work and drive success in the global marketplace.

Chapter 12: Measuring Success in Remote Work

As organizations embrace remote work, it becomes essential to establish metrics for measuring success. This chapter explores the key performance indicators (KPIs) and metrics that organizations can use to evaluate the effectiveness of remote work and its impact on business outcomes.

1. Defining Success in Remote Work

Success in remote work can encompass various dimensions, including employee performance, engagement, productivity, and overall satisfaction. Organizations must define what success looks like in their specific context.

Setting Clear Objectives

Establishing clear objectives and expectations for remote teams is crucial. Organizations should identify the key outcomes they want to achieve and align their performance metrics accordingly.

For example, a remote sales team may define success in terms of meeting quarterly sales targets and maintaining customer satisfaction scores. "Having clear objectives keeps us focused and motivated to deliver results," shares Tom, a sales representative.

2. Tracking Employee Performance

To evaluate employee performance effectively, organizations can utilize various tools and techniques. Performance management systems can track individual contributions and provide insights into overall team performance.

Implementing Performance Dashboards

Performance dashboards can offer real-time insights into individual and team performance. These dashboards can display key metrics, such as project completion rates, deadlines met, and quality of work.

A remote project management firm utilizes performance dashboards to track project progress and individual contributions, allowing managers to identify areas for improvement and recognize high performers. "Having access to performance metrics helps us celebrate achievements and address challenges proactively," notes Lisa, a project manager.

3. Measuring Employee Engagement

Employee engagement is a critical factor in remote work success. Organizations should regularly assess employee engagement levels to gauge satisfaction, commitment, and overall morale.

Conducting Engagement Surveys

Regular employee engagement surveys can provide valuable insights into how remote workers feel about their roles, company culture, and support from leadership. Analyzing survey results allows organizations to identify trends and areas for improvement.

A remote tech company conducts quarterly engagement surveys, using the feedback to implement initiatives that enhance employee satisfaction. "Listening to our employees' voices helps us create a positive work environment," shares Rachel, an HR manager.

4. Evaluating Productivity Metrics

Measuring productivity in a remote work environment requires a shift in focus from hours worked to outcomes achieved. Organizations should identify productivity metrics that align with their goals.

Identifying Key Productivity Indicators

Key productivity indicators may include project completion rates, client satisfaction scores, and time spent on value-added tasks. Tracking these metrics allows organizations to assess the effectiveness of their remote work strategies.

For instance, a remote consulting firm measures productivity based on the number of successful client engagements and project deliverables completed within set timelines. "Focusing on outcomes rather than hours worked has helped us understand our true productivity," notes Eric, a consultant.

5. Analyzing Overall Business Impact

To measure the overall impact of remote work on the organization, companies should analyze key business outcomes, such as revenue growth, employee retention rates, and client satisfaction.

Linking Remote Work to Business Goals

Organizations should establish a clear connection between remote work practices and their business goals. Regularly reviewing business metrics in relation to remote work initiatives can help identify areas of success and opportunities for improvement.

A remote marketing agency tracks revenue growth and client retention rates alongside its remote work policies, demonstrating the positive impact of remote work on overall business performance. "Seeing the correlation between our remote practices and business success reinforces our commitment to this model," shares Sarah, the agency's CEO.

Conclusion

Measuring success in remote work is essential for organizations to evaluate their effectiveness and make informed decisions. By defining success, tracking employee performance, measuring engagement, evaluating productivity metrics, and analyzing overall business impact, organizations can optimize their remote work strategies and drive continuous improvement.

Chapter 13: Building a Remote Work Culture

In a world where teams are dispersed across various locations, creating a strong remote work culture is vital for fostering collaboration, engagement, and a sense of belonging. This chapter explores the elements necessary to build and maintain a robust remote work culture.

1. Defining Company Values in a Remote Context

Establishing clear company values is essential for guiding behavior and decision-making within a remote work environment. Organizations must ensure that their values resonate with all employees, regardless of where they work.

Aligning Values with Remote Work Practices

Values should not only be aspirational but also actionable. For instance, if a company values innovation, it should encourage remote employees to share ideas and take risks, fostering an environment where creativity thrives.

A global tech firm emphasizes its commitment to innovation by hosting regular virtual hackathons, inviting employees from different locations to collaborate on new ideas. "These events bring our values to life and spark creativity across the globe," shares Mia, the innovation lead.

2. Fostering Communication and Transparency

Open communication is crucial for maintaining trust and transparency within remote teams. Organizations should prioritize creating channels for honest and regular communication.

Utilizing Diverse Communication Tools

Different tools can facilitate various types of communication—synchronous and asynchronous. Video conferencing can be used for real-time discussions, while chat platforms allow for ongoing conversations and quick check-ins.

A remote consulting firm uses a mix of video calls for team meetings and a chat platform for daily updates. "Having diverse communication tools helps us stay connected and informed," explains Ahmed, a team leader.

3. Encouraging Social Interaction and Team Building

Remote work can lead to feelings of isolation, making it essential for organizations to encourage social interactions among team members.

Implementing Virtual Team Building Activities

Virtual team-building activities can enhance relationships and promote camaraderie among remote workers. These may include virtual coffee breaks, game nights, and collaborative challenges.

A remote marketing agency organizes bi-monthly virtual game nights to strengthen team bonds and foster a sense of community. "These activities create an informal space for us to connect and have fun," shares Laura, a marketing specialist.

4. Recognizing and Celebrating Achievements

Recognition is a powerful motivator, especially in a remote work environment where employees may feel disconnected from the organization's successes.

Developing a Recognition Program

Organizations should establish formal recognition programs that acknowledge individual and team contributions. This can include awards, shout-outs in team meetings, or features in company newsletters.

A remote financial services firm implements a "kudos" system where employees can publicly recognize their peers for outstanding work. "Recognizing each other's achievements boosts morale and encourages a positive culture," notes James, a compliance officer.

5. Providing Opportunities for Professional Development

Investing in employee growth and development is crucial for maintaining engagement and satisfaction in a remote work environment.

Creating Accessible Learning Opportunities

Organizations should offer accessible learning and development resources, such as online courses, webinars, and mentorship programs. Encouraging employees to pursue their interests and expand their skill sets benefits both the individual and the organization.

A remote tech company partners with online learning platforms to provide employees with access to a wide range of courses. "Having the opportunity to learn and grow keeps me motivated and engaged," shares Rachel, a software developer.

Conclusion

Building a strong remote work culture requires intentional effort and commitment from both leadership and employees. By defining company values, fostering communication and transparency, encouraging social interactions, recognizing achievements, and providing professional development opportunities, organizations can cultivate a thriving remote work culture that supports engagement, collaboration, and innovation.

Chapter 14: The Role of Technology in Enhancing Remote Work

Technology serves as the backbone of remote work, enabling teams to collaborate, communicate, and maintain productivity regardless of physical location. This chapter explores the critical role of technology in enhancing remote work experiences.

1. Choosing the Right Tools for Collaboration

Selecting the right collaboration tools is essential for facilitating effective teamwork and communication in a remote setting. Organizations must assess their needs and choose tools that align with their objectives.

Evaluating Collaboration Platforms

Different collaboration platforms offer various features—some focus on project management, while others prioritize communication. Organizations should evaluate their workflows and select tools that enhance productivity.

For example, a remote design firm utilizes tools like Trello for project management and Slack for team communication, ensuring seamless collaboration. "Having the right tools in place makes our workflow more efficient," notes Emma, a project manager.

2. Implementing Cloud-Based Solutions

Cloud-based solutions provide remote teams with access to essential documents and resources from anywhere, promoting flexibility and collaboration.

Leveraging Cloud Storage and File Sharing

Organizations should utilize cloud storage solutions that facilitate easy file sharing and collaboration on documents.

Tools like Google Drive and Dropbox enable real-time editing and ensure that team members are always working on the latest version.

A remote consulting firm uses Google Workspace for document collaboration, allowing multiple team members to work on projects simultaneously. "The ability to collaborate in real time has transformed our workflow," shares Eric, a consultant.

3. Enhancing Communication with Video Conferencing

Video conferencing tools play a crucial role in fostering face-to-face interactions among remote team members. Regular video calls can enhance engagement and strengthen relationships.

Best Practices for Effective Video Conferencing

Organizations should establish best practices for video calls, including setting clear agendas, ensuring technical readiness, and encouraging participation from all team members. This creates a more productive and engaging environment.

A remote sales team holds weekly video check-ins to discuss progress and challenges. "These meetings help us stay aligned and connected," notes Tom, a sales representative.

4. Utilizing Project Management Software

Project management software is essential for tracking progress, assigning tasks, and ensuring accountability within remote teams.

Setting Up a Structured Project Management System

Organizations should implement a project management system that offers visibility into project timelines, deadlines, and individual responsibilities. This helps teams stay organized and focused on their goals.

A remote marketing agency uses Asana to manage projects, allowing team members to track progress and deadlines. "Having a structured system keeps us accountable and on track," shares Sarah, the agency's project manager.

5. Ensuring Data Security and Compliance

As remote work relies heavily on technology, ensuring data security and compliance is paramount. Organizations must implement measures to protect sensitive information.

Implementing Cybersecurity Protocols

Organizations should develop and communicate cybersecurity protocols that outline best practices for data protection. This may include training employees on password management, phishing awareness, and secure data handling.

A remote financial services firm conducts regular cybersecurity training sessions to educate employees about potential threats and how to mitigate risks. "Staying informed about cybersecurity is crucial for our clients' trust," shares James, a compliance officer.

Conclusion

Technology plays a vital role in enhancing remote work experiences and enabling organizations to thrive in a distributed environment. By choosing the right tools for collaboration, implementing cloud-based solutions, enhancing communication with video conferencing, utilizing project management software, and ensuring data security, organizations can optimize their remote work strategies and foster productivity and engagement.

Chapter 15: Remote Work and Employee Well-Being

Employee well-being is a critical consideration in the remote work landscape. Organizations must prioritize mental, emotional, and physical health to support their employees in a virtual environment. This chapter explores strategies for promoting well-being among remote workers.

1. Understanding the Challenges of Remote Work

While remote work offers flexibility, it also presents unique challenges that can impact employee well-being. Isolation, blurred boundaries between work and personal life, and increased screen time can lead to stress and burnout.

Identifying Common Well-Being Concerns

Organizations should conduct assessments to identify common well-being concerns among remote employees. Understanding these challenges allows organizations to implement targeted interventions.

A remote tech company conducts regular surveys to gauge employee well-being and gather feedback on their experiences. "Listening to our employees helps us understand their needs and challenges," shares Rachel, the HR manager.

2. Promoting Work-Life Balance

Encouraging work-life balance is essential for preventing burnout and enhancing overall well-being. Organizations should set clear expectations regarding working hours and encourage employees to prioritize self-care.

Establishing Clear Boundaries

Organizations can promote work-life balance by establishing guidelines around work hours and encouraging employees to disconnect after work. This may include implementing "no meeting" days or flexible schedules.

A remote consulting firm emphasizes the importance of work-life balance by encouraging employees to set boundaries and take regular breaks. "Having the freedom to manage my schedule has significantly improved my well-being," notes Eric, a consultant.

3. Offering Mental Health Resources

Mental health support is crucial for remote employees, as the isolation of remote work can lead to increased feelings of anxiety and stress. Organizations should offer accessible mental health resources.

Implementing Employee Assistance Programs

Employee assistance programs (EAPs) provide confidential support for employees facing mental health challenges. Organizations should ensure that employees are aware of these resources and how to access them.

A remote marketing agency offers an EAP that includes counseling services and mental health resources. "Knowing that support is available makes a big difference," shares Laura, a marketing specialist.

4. Encouraging Physical Well-Being

Physical well-being is equally important for overall health. Organizations should promote healthy habits and provide resources for maintaining physical fitness.

Implementing Wellness Initiatives

Organizations can implement wellness initiatives that encourage physical activity, such as virtual fitness challenges, gym memberships, or access to online workout classes.

A remote tech company organizes monthly fitness challenges to promote physical well-being among employees. "Participating in fitness challenges has helped me stay active and connected with my colleagues," notes Jenna, a software engineer.

5. Fostering Social Connections

Social connections are vital for employee well-being. Organizations should create opportunities for employees to connect and build relationships, even in a virtual setting.

Creating Social Platforms for Interaction

Organizations can create dedicated social platforms for informal interactions, such as virtual coffee breaks, book clubs, or interest-based groups. These platforms foster camaraderie and help employees feel more connected.

A remote financial services firm hosts regular virtual coffee breaks where employees can socialize and discuss non-work-related topics. "Having a space to connect with colleagues makes remote work feel less isolating," shares James, a compliance officer.

Conclusion

Promoting employee well-being in a remote work environment requires a comprehensive approach that addresses mental, emotional, and physical health. By understanding the challenges of remote work, promoting work-life balance, offering mental health resources, encouraging physical well-being, and fostering social connections, organizations can create a supportive environment that enhances employee satisfaction and productivity.

Chapter 16: The Future of Remote Work

As remote work continues to evolve, organizations must prepare for the future of work and adapt their strategies to thrive in an ever-changing landscape. This chapter explores emerging trends and predictions for the future of remote work.

1. The Hybrid Work Model

The hybrid work model, which combines remote and in-office work, is becoming increasingly popular. Organizations are recognizing the benefits of flexibility while maintaining a physical presence.

Designing Flexible Work Environments

Organizations should design flexible work environments that accommodate both remote and in-office employees. This may include reconfiguring office spaces to facilitate collaboration and integrating technology for seamless communication.

A global marketing agency adopts a hybrid work model, allowing employees to choose their work location while providing collaborative spaces in the office. "The hybrid model gives us the best of both worlds," notes Sarah, the agency's project manager.

2. Advancements in Technology and Automation

Technological advancements will continue to shape the future of remote work. Automation, artificial intelligence, and machine learning will streamline processes and enhance productivity.

Embracing Innovative Technologies

Organizations should stay abreast of emerging technologies and explore how they can integrate these innovations into their remote work strategies. This may include adopting AI tools for project management or utilizing automation to enhance efficiency.

A remote consulting firm implements AI-powered project management software to optimize workflows and allocate resources more effectively. "Embracing technology has transformed how we operate," shares Eric, a consultant.

3. Focus on Diversity and Inclusion

Diversity and inclusion will remain paramount in the future of remote work. Organizations must prioritize building diverse teams and fostering inclusive practices.

Implementing Inclusive Recruitment Strategies

Organizations should implement inclusive recruitment strategies to attract diverse talent from various backgrounds. This may include revising job descriptions, utilizing diverse recruitment platforms, and promoting an inclusive culture.

A remote tech company actively seeks diverse candidates by partnering with organizations that focus on underrepresented groups in tech. "Building a diverse team enriches our perspectives and drives innovation," notes Mia, the innovation lead.

4. Emphasis on Employee Well-Being

The emphasis on employee well-being will continue to grow as organizations recognize the importance of mental, emotional, and physical health in enhancing productivity and engagement.

Prioritizing Comprehensive Well-Being Programs

Organizations should prioritize comprehensive well-being programs that address the holistic needs of employees. This includes mental health resources, wellness initiatives, and opportunities for social connection.

A remote financial services firm invests in comprehensive well-being programs, providing access to mental health resources and fitness challenges. "Taking care of our employees' well-being is essential for our success," shares James, a compliance officer.

5. Evolving Leadership Practices

Leadership practices will evolve to accommodate the remote work environment. Leaders must develop skills that foster trust, collaboration, and engagement among remote teams.

Investing in Leadership Development

Organizations should invest in leadership development programs that equip leaders with the skills needed to navigate the complexities of remote work. This includes training on communication, emotional intelligence, and conflict resolution.

A remote marketing agency offers leadership development workshops focused on remote team management. "Equipping our leaders with the right skills is crucial for our success," notes Sarah, the agency's project manager.

Conclusion

The future of remote work presents both opportunities and challenges for organizations. By embracing hybrid work models, advancing technology, focusing on diversity and inclusion, prioritizing employee well-being, and evolving leadership practices, organizations can position themselves for success in the dynamic landscape of remote work.

Chapter 17: Conclusion: Embracing the New Era of Work

As we conclude our exploration of remote work, it is clear that this paradigm shift has transformed how we perceive and approach work. The rise of remote work represents a new era of freedom, flexibility, and opportunity for organizations and employees alike. This chapter reflects on key insights and encourages readers to embrace the future of work.

1. Reflecting on the Journey

The transition to remote work has been a journey filled with challenges and successes. Organizations have had to adapt their strategies, invest in technology, and prioritize employee well-being to navigate this new landscape.

Lessons Learned from Remote Work

Throughout this journey, valuable lessons have emerged, including the importance of communication, the need for flexibility, and the significance of fostering a strong remote work culture. Organizations that embrace these lessons will thrive in the evolving work environment.

2. The Benefits of Remote Work

Remote work offers numerous benefits, including increased flexibility, improved work-life balance, and access to a diverse talent pool. These advantages contribute to enhanced employee satisfaction and productivity, creating a win-win situation for organizations and employees.

Recognizing the Value of Flexibility

Flexibility is a defining characteristic of remote work, allowing employees to tailor their schedules to fit their needs. Organizations that prioritize flexibility will attract and retain top talent in a competitive job market.

3. Overcoming Challenges

While remote work presents many advantages, it is not without its challenges. Organizations must address issues such as communication barriers, feelings of isolation, and maintaining engagement among remote teams.

Commitment to Continuous Improvement

Organizations should remain committed to continuous improvement by regularly assessing their remote work practices, gathering feedback from employees, and implementing necessary changes. This commitment will ensure that remote work evolves to meet the needs of employees and the organization.

4. Embracing the Future of Work

As we look ahead, the future of work will continue to evolve. Organizations must remain agile and open to embracing new trends, technologies, and practices that will shape the way we work.

Anticipating Change and Adaptation

By anticipating change and adapting to new developments, organizations can position themselves for success in the ever-changing work landscape. Embracing innovation and fostering a culture of continuous learning will be key to thriving in the future.

5. A Call to Action

In closing, organizations and individuals alike are encouraged to embrace the new era of work. By adopting a proactive mindset, prioritizing well-being, and fostering collaboration, we can create a future of work that is not only productive but also fulfilling.

Together, We Can Thrive

As we navigate this exciting journey, let us remember that the future of work is a collective effort. By working together, supporting one another, and embracing change, we can thrive in this new era of freedom and opportunity.

Overall Conclusion

The rise of remote work marks a transformative shift in how we approach our professional lives. This new era of flexibility, autonomy, and innovation has empowered individuals and organizations to adapt to changing circumstances while reimagining the traditional workplace. Throughout this eBook, we have explored the multifaceted nature of remote work, examining its benefits, challenges, and the strategies that can help individuals and teams thrive in this evolving landscape.

As organizations embrace remote work, they are discovering that the benefits extend far beyond mere convenience. Enhanced productivity, improved work-life balance, and access to a diverse talent pool are just a few of the advantages that come with this paradigm shift. However, as we've discussed, the journey to successful remote work requires intentional effort in fostering a strong culture, leveraging technology, prioritizing employee well-being, and adapting leadership practices.

The future of work is filled with opportunities for growth, innovation, and connection. By remaining agile and responsive to change, organizations can create environments where employees feel valued, supported, and engaged. Embracing diversity, inclusion, and well-being will be key to building resilient teams that can navigate the complexities of the modern workplace.

As we move forward into this new era, let us remain committed to fostering collaboration, nurturing relationships, and leveraging the unique advantages that remote work offers. Together, we can shape a future of work that not only meets the demands of today but also paves the way for continued success in the years to come.

References

Bai, X., & Wang, X. (2021). "Remote work in the post-pandemic era: Challenges and opportunities." Journal of Business Research, 129, 638-648. DOI:10.1016/j.jbusres.2021.02.015

Bourke, J., & Dillon, B. (2021). "The diversity and inclusion revolution: Eight powerful truths." Deloitte Insights. Retrieved from Deloitte

Cascio, W. F., & Montealegre, R. (2016). "How technology is changing work and organizations." Annual Review of Organizational Psychology and Organizational Behavior, 3(1), 349-375. DOI:10.1146/annurev-orgpsych-032315-025022

Gallup. (2021). "State of the Global Workplace: 2021 Report." Retrieved from Gallup

Graham, M., & Hutton, W. (2021). "Remote Work and the Future of Work: The Pandemic and Beyond." Social Research: An International Quarterly, 88(3), 677-694.

Luthans, F., & Youssef, C. M. (2007). "Emerging Positive Organizational Behavior." Journal of Management, 33(3), 321-349. DOI:10.1177/0149206307300814

Mann, S., & Holdsworth, L. (2003). "The role of work-life balance in the future of work." International Journal of Human Resource Management, 14(3), 525-543. DOI:10.1080/0958519032000051201

Prasad, A., & Prasad, P. (2021). "How to Thrive in a Remote Work Environment." Harvard Business Review. Retrieved from HBR

Raghuram, S., & Wiesenfeld, B. M. (2004). "Work–Family Conflict and Career Outcomes: A Study of the Work–Family Interface." Journal of Applied Psychology, 89(5), 1128-1137. DOI:10.1037/0021-9010.89.5.1128

Schmidt, G., & Chao, K. J. (2022). "The Hybrid Workplace: How to Make it Work." McKinsey & Company. Retrieved from McKinsey

Turetken, O., & Ozturk, M. (2022). "Managing remote teams: A systematic review of the literature." International Journal of Project Management, 40(3), 207-221. DOI:10.1016/j.ijproman.2021.07.002

www.ingramcontent.com/pod-product-compliance
Lightning Source LLC
Chambersburg PA
CBHW070349230526
45471CB00006B/2480